With Na... ...h.
and cler... ...en
A Faun a-peeping through the green,
and felt the Classics were not dead,
To glimpse a naiad's reedy head,
Or hear the Goat-foot piping low:.....
But these are things I do not know.
I only know that you may lie
Daylong and watch the Cambridge sky,
and, flower-lulled in sleepy grass,
Hear the cool lapse of hours pass,
Until the centuries blend and blur
In Grantchester, in Grantchester......
Still in the dawnlit waters cool
His ghostly Lordship swims his pool,
And tries the strokes, essays the tricks,
Long learnt on Hellespont, or Styx.
Dan Chaucer hears his river still
Chatter beneath a phantom mill.
Tennyson notes, with studious eye,
How Cambridge waters hurry by......
And in that garden, black and white,
Creep whispers through the grass all night;
And spectral dance, before the dawn,
A hundred Vicars down the lawn;
Curates, long dust, will come and go,
On lissom, clerical, printless toe;
And oft betwixt the boughs is seen
The sly shade of a Rural Dean......
Till, at a shiver in the skies,
Vanishing with Satanic cries,
The prim ecclesiastic rout
Leaves but a startled sleeper-out,
Grey heavens, the first birds' drowsy calls,
The falling house that never falls.

God! I will pack, and take a train,

To Mary Ellen and Phillip

RUPERT BROOKE

AND

THE OLD VICARAGE, GRANTCHESTER

With all good wishes

Mary Archer

September 2002

RUPERT BROOKE

AND

THE OLD VICARAGE, GRANTCHESTER

DR. MARY D. ARCHER

with drawings by Nevill Willmer

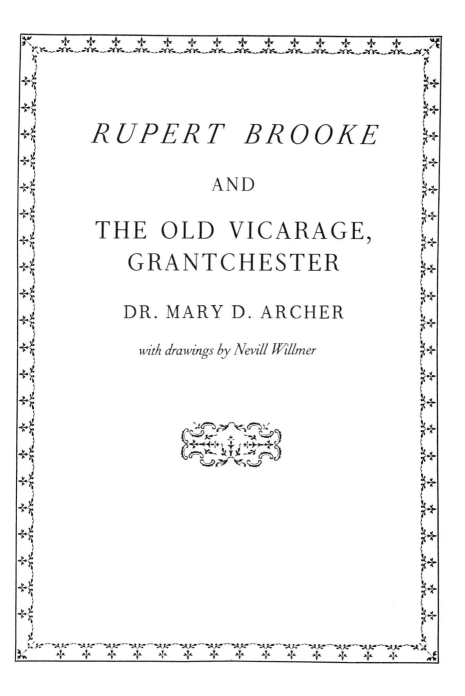

All royalties from the sale of this book go to the parish
church of St Andrew and St Mary, Grantchester

Frontispiece: The Old Vicarage, c. 1910.

First published in Great Britain 1989
by Silent Books, Cambridge CB4 5RA
Reprinted 1992, 1994, 2001
© copyright Mary Archer 1989
pencil drawings © copyright Nevill Willmer 1989
this edition © copyright Silent Books 1989
© Photographs of Rupert Brooke reproduced
by permission of King's College Library, Cambridge
Manuscript facsimile copyright © The Brooke Trust 1989

Photograph of the Old Vicarage reproduced by
permission of Rugby School
© Wood engraving by Gwen Raverat reproduced by
permission of Sophie Gurney

New photographs by Ray Kimberly

ISBN 1 85183 007 3

Typeset by Goodfellow & Egan, Cambridge
Printed in Great Britain by
St Edmundsbury Press, Bury St Edmunds, Suffolk

PREFACE

MANY people come to Grantchester in search of the spirit of Rupert Brooke or to learn more of the connexion between the village, the poet and one of his best-loved poems, *The Old Vicarage, Grantchester*. This small book is intended to help them in their quest. The aim has been to sketch the history of the house, to give an impression of Brooke and the circumstances in which he wrote the poem, and to relate the poem to the house, the river and the village.

This account has evolved from a talk which I, who have the good fortune to live in the 'reverend dream', gave in Grantchester Village Hall on 3 August 1987, the centenary to the day of Brooke's birth. Professor Nevill Willmer of Yew Garth, Grantchester suggested to me that I should prepare a written version, and this is it. I am indebted to Nevill for his encouragement, his delightful drawings and for drafting much of the material on Brooke's early life, in which we have made liberal use of the biographies of Brooke by Christopher Hassall and John Lehmann. Nevill's conversations with George Rogers and Bill Clamp have provided valuable information on life in Grantchester in Brooke's time, and we have drawn on *A History of Grantchester* by S. P. Widnall, also undertaken to aid the funds of the parish church.

I thank Bird's Farm Publications for permission to quote from *The New Heritage* and to use material from *Old Grantchester* by Nevill Willmer, and *Punch* and the *Cambridge Evening News* for permission to quote from the parodies by Roger Woddis and Robert Smith respectively. I gratefully acknowledge the help of the following persons: Dr M. A. Halls, Archivist of King's College, for help with the Brooke archive and the clue to 'Mr Shuckburgh'; Mr D. K. Holbrook and Mr Lionel Munby for the tale of Madingley on Christmas Eve; Mrs J. Macrory, Librarian of Rugby School, for the loan of a photograph from Brooke's album showing the Old

Vicarage *c.* 1910; Mrs Cyril Neeve for information about her late husband's family; Professor R. I. Page for comments on the early links between Corpus Christi College and Grantchester church; Mr M. J. Petty, Librarian of the Cambridgeshire Collection, for an introduction to 'The Knocking Ghost of Barton' and historical material on the Old Vicarage; Miss Alison Taylor, County Archaeologist, for access to archaeological records of the village. Finally I thank Dr G. H. W. Rylands, Professor J. H. Stallworthy and Professor J. E. Stevens for their kindly and scholarly criticisms and emendations of successive versions of the text.

MARY ARCHER

The Old Vicarage, Grantchester
September 1988

A commercial postcard, published after Brooke's death, wrongly identifying the Old Vicarage as his house.

GRANTCHESTER, like most Cambridgeshire villages, is an ancient settlement: all along the river Granta, crop marks reveal scattered Iron Age settlements. Cambridge itself, although on the margin of Fenland, has long been important in that it stood at the head of the navigable river and at the foot of its fordable reach. On the high ground of the Castle Hill area of the city there was a fortified Iron Age village, and Grantchester too shows traces of Iron Age settlement. In Roman times more settlements were established on the East Anglian rivers; in Cambridge a fort was built on the site of the Iron Age settlement and a wooden bridge close to the modern site of Magdalene Bridge: hence Cambridge's early name 'Grante-brycge' as an alternative to 'Grantacaestir'. Roman remains have also been found in Grantchester in the field south of Manor Farm. In early Anglo-Saxon times, Cambridge briefly reverted to scattered peasant settlements and Grantchester may have assumed greater relative importance, for traces of a *grubenhaus*, a sixth-century dwelling, were found in the 1971 excavation of the bumpy land

Grantchester, Rupert Brooke's House

behind the old school and the Red Lion public house which marks the heart of the ancient village. The Anglo-Saxon name of the village, 'Grantasete', means 'the settlers by the Granta'. But by the ninth century, the pre-eminence of Cambridge had been assured by its importance as a trading and administrative centre, and was later to be enhanced by the development of the university.

The earliest church in Grantchester, which stood on the site of the present church, was Saxon. This was pulled down by the Normans, who built themselves a new one, of which there remains only the core of the north wall of the nave. Church records date from 1280, and the present church is mostly fourteenth and fifteenth century, although it incorporates several earlier fragments. The earliest recorded incumbents were Rectors; that is, they lived off the greater tithes received from the local farms. Thomas de Eltislee, who was the first Master of Corpus Christi College, was installed as Rector of Grantchester in 1363. The college purchased the Rectory in 1380 for the sum of 500 marks and became Patron of the Living. Subsequent incumbents, by preference Fellows of the college, took the title of Vicar of Grantchester.

The early incumbents probably lived in a rectory which was not far from the church, near the end of what is now Burnt Close. This rectory seems to have been demolished in the early seventeenth century; the hollow ground which marked it was filled in early this century. The house with which we are concerned, now called the Old Vicarage, was built on the site of a previous building shortly before 1685, for an ecclesiastical visitation of that year refers to a 'good, new built Vicaridge House'. It was used as the Grantchester vicarage until the early nineteenth century. At the time of the enclosures, the then Vicar, William Butts (incumbent 1778–1806), was listed as resident in the house, which was known at that time as Vicarage Homestead. But the next incumbent, John Hewitt (1806–1850), who also had charge of the parish of Willingham, cannot have lived in the house for long since, in the *Cambridge Chronicle* of 3 August 1828, it was advertised to be let, and in Romilly's Cambridge Diary of 1836 it is mentioned that some members of the Lilley family moved to the Vicarage in or around 1836; they probably lived in it until the death of Edward Lilley (who owned the nearby Manor Farm) in 1836.

In 1850 Grantchester's new incumbent, William Martin, declined to live in the Old Vicarage on account of its dampness and its lack of stables, and a handsome Victorian house was built for him in what is now Vicarage Drive, near the site of the old rectory and the church. This house in its turn has recently ceased to be the vicarage; renamed *The Glebe*, it is now privately owned. The present vicarage is the modern house by the gate to the church.

In 1853 the Old Vicarage was bought by Samuel Page Widnall, whose father was a local market gardener famed for his dahlias, which he grew in extensive nurseries in the grounds now occupied

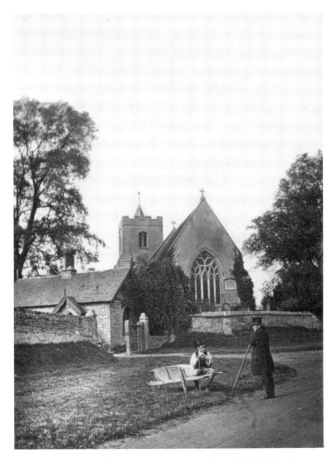

Grantchester Church photographed by S. P. Widnall.

by Riversdale, the large house opposite the Old Vicarage. Widnall, who lived in the Old Vicarage until his death in 1894, was a keen photographer and a skilful maker of models; his model of the church can be seen in the vestry, and that of the Old Mill in the Cambridge Folk Museum. He was also something of a local

S. P. Widnall with family and friends by the verandah at the rear of the Old Vicarage. . . .

. . . .and in the garden by the fountain.

GRANTCHESTER, CAMBS.

(2 Miles from the Town of Cambridge.)

Sale of a Valuable

Freehold and Copyhold Estate

Comprising the

OLD VICARAGE HOUSE

with old world garden and outbuildings, containing in all 1 Acre, 0 Roods, 32 Poles, in the occupation of Mr. H. R. Neeve.

A DWELLING HOUSE

with garden, Store rooms and Stabling in the occupation of Mr. J. W. Stevenson.

A Valuable Enclosure of

Old PASTURE LAND

containing about 1 Acre with a long frontage to the High road, very suitable for building purposes.

A Claybat, Brick and Slated Cottage

with Garden and Out-houses, in the occupation of Mr. J. Richardson.

A SUPERIOR RESIDENCE

with large Garden and Out-houses, known as "Yew Garth," in the occupation of C. Warburton, Esq.   A Valuable Close of

PASTURE LAND

known as "The Orchard," thickly planted with choice fruit trees, containing 1 Acre, 2 Roods, 4 Poles, with a frontage to the High Road of 320 feet, ripe for immediate development. The whole-producing an annual rental of

£110 - 0s. - 0d.

MESSRS. CHALK

are Instructed by Mrs. Giles to Sell the above by Auction in Six Lots,

On Saturday, May 30th, 1914

At 4.30 o'clock in the Afternoon, at the

LION HOTEL, PETTY CURY, CAMBRIDGE.

Particulars may be obtained of **H. E. Ellis, Esq.**, Solicitor, Hemel Hempstead; or of the Auctioneers, 11, Alexandra Street, Cambridge, and Linton, Cambs.

Widnall's Castle Ruin, now called the Folly and used as an office.

historian. His book on Grantchester, produced in 1875, was not only written but also printed by him on his own press, which occupied a shed off the kitchen of the Old Vicarage. His most ambitious project was perhaps to build the 'Castle Ruin', the clunch folly in Gothic revival style at the end of the garden near the Mill Stream.

On Widnall's death, the house passed to his sister-in-law Sarah (Lally) Smith, and then on her death in 1908 to a niece, Mrs Emily Giles, along with the five other properties in Widnall's estate in Grantchester. Mrs Giles never lived in the house, but installed as tenants Henry and Florence Neeve and their son Cyril; Henry Neeve was a carpenter employed by the well-known Cambridge contractor Arthur Negus. In 1914 Mrs Giles sold Widnall's estate in

Florence and Henry Neeve and their son Cyril.

six lots. The Old Vicarage was bought by J. W. Stevenson, who at the same time bought the Orchard next door, of which he was already the tenant. Henry Neeve continued to live in the Old Vicarage until the end of the decade. It was in his time that Rupert Brooke entered the story of the house; he first took lodgings in Grantchester with the Stevensons at the Orchard in 1909, when he graduated from King's College, Cambridge, and then from 1910 to 1912 with the Neeves at the Old Vicarage.

Brooke came to Grantchester a somewhat disappointed man. Until the summer of 1909, his schooling had flowed smoothly and with some distinction. He was born on 3 August 1887, the second son of William Parker Brooke, then housemaster of School Field at Rugby School (and, incidentally, the first non-Etonian Fellow of

Rupert Brooke, 1906.

King's). Probably because of frequent illness, Rupert was first sent to Hillbrow, a preparatory school in Rugby, at the rather late age of ten; James Strachey and Duncan Grant (who was James's cousin) were among his contemporaries there. In 1901 Brooke entered Rugby School and lived with the other boarders in School Field, then noted for its strict discipline under 'Tooler' Brooke and Ma Tooler. Among Brooke's close friends in the house was Geoffrey Keynes, later a distinguished surgeon and bibliographer, one of the four literary trustees appointed in Mrs Brooke's will, and editor of the standard edition of *The Poetical Works*.

Brooke moved up through Rugby on the classical side but showed an early interest, fostered by St John Welles Lucas-Lucas, in poetry. He read a paper on Swinburne to the sixth-form literary society, started a literary supplement, *The Phoenix*, to the school magazine, and won the school poetry prize with his dramatic poem *The Bastille*. He also won several prizes in the poetry competitions run by the *Westminster Gazette*. In addition to these literary pursuits, Brooke took an active part in school sport, playing rugby football in the first XV and cricket in the XI. His school career was crowned by a classical scholarship to King's in December 1905 and he went up in Michaelmas Term 1906.

Brooke's school friendships bore fruit at Cambridge. Under the patronage of Lytton Strachey (elder brother of James) and Maynard

Keynes (elder brother of Geoffrey), Brooke was elected to the exclusive and secret intellectual society known as the Apostles. Through early friendships at Hillbrow and Rugby and his circle at King's, Brooke also became involved with the Bloomsbury set, whom he eventually came to distrust and dislike.

Early in his Cambridge career, Rupert met his namesake Justin Brooke of Emmanuel – no relation but a member of the Brooke Bond Teas family – and a bond of friendship based on mutual love of the theatre developed between them. Through Justin, Rupert was given a walk-on part as the Herald in the 1906 Greek Play *Eumenides* at the A.D.C. theatre. 'I put a long horn to my lips and pretend to blow,' he reported to Lucas, 'and a villain in the orchestra simultaneously wantons on the cornet. It is very symbolical.' In the audience at one of the performances and much struck by the appearance of the Herald was another Apostle, Edward Marsh, later to be Brooke's mentor, early biographer and literary executor.

The next theatrical production in which both Brookes were involved was Christopher Marlowe's *Dr. Faustus*. This they produced independently of the official A.D.C. and, after it, they founded the Marlowe Dramatic Society, which had as its main aim the production of early English plays, in the footsteps of William Poel and the Elizabethan Stage Society. Rupert became the first President and Geoffrey Keynes, by that time a science exhibitioner at Pembroke, the Secretary. Its first venture, a response to an approach to Justin by the Master of Christ's College, was initially planned to be an outdoor production of *Comus* in the college gardens to mark the tercentenary of Milton's birth; in the event it was staged in the New Theatre. During its gestation period, Rupert was brought into contact with a circle of Cambridge people later dubbed the Neo-Pagans – Francis and Frances Cornford, Jacques Raverat and Gwen Darwin among them – who later became distinguished in the fields of literature and art. *Comus* was regarded by its critics as no more than a moderate success, but it made history in that it was the first undergraduate production in which women took part.

Besides these theatrical interests, Brooke had made friends in King's with his fellow freshman Hugh Dalton (later a Labour

Brooke reciting to Dudley Ward and Jacques Raverat, the Old Vicarage, 1911.

Chancellor of the Exchequer) and through him had been attracted by Socialism and the Fabians. He joined the Cambridge University Fabian Society, eventually becoming its President, and through the Fabians became a friend of Dudley Ward of St John's, with whose family he stayed in Somerset in the summer of 1909.

The Fabian Society had just admitted women members of Newnham and Girton Colleges. Katharine (Ka) Cox and Margery Olivier were among the first of those to be admitted, and at a dinner of the society just before the production of *Comus*, Rupert met Noel Olivier, Margery's younger sister and still a schoolgirl. The two girls, Ka and Noel, very different in age, character and interests, affected Rupert deeply. Whether *post hoc* or *propter hoc* we do not know, but Rupert failed to get the First in the Classical Tripos at which he had aimed and which his mother had expected.

His tutor was sympathetic and advised Brooke to turn to English for work towards obtaining a Fellowship, also suggesting that he should move away from Cambridge and its distractions. It was for that reason that, in a rather turbulent state of mind, Brooke came to lodge in Grantchester at the age of twenty-two. To atone for his indifferent performance in the Tripos, he worked hard for two University prizes for which he had entered, the Charles Oldham Shakespeare Scholarship and the Harness Essay Prize. For the first his subject was John Webster, Elizabethan dramatist and poet, and for the second, Puritanism and the early English drama. He won

In the front garden of the Orchard, Grantchester 1910.

both prizes, and also several other literary competitions. Brooke's father died at the beginning of 1910 and his mother summoned him home to act as temporary housemaster at School Field, which kept him away from Grantchester for the whole of that Lent term.

In the summer of 1910, during a tour in the West Country with Dudley Ward to promote Fabianism, Rupert met Noel Olivier in Hampshire and the two entered into a secret engagement. This considerably complicated relations both with his mother and with Ka, whom he later ardently pursued only to reject her when she eventually responded.

Brooke's first rooms in Grantchester were in the Orchard, a house forming part of the original complex of farm buildings associated with the Old Vicarage. He lodged in the slate-roofed part of the house nearest the corner of the road. (The part with a pantile roof was then an appleloft above and a stable below.) 'I'm in a

Brooke on the river with Dudley Ward.

small house, a sort of cottage,' he reported to his cousin Erica Cotterill, 'The room I have opens straight out onto a stone verandah covered with creepers, & a little old garden full of old-fashioned flowers and *crammed* with roses.' Mr Stevenson, the owner of the Orchard, was a dairyman who, with his wife and daughters, managed the Tea Garden which was open to the public in the summer and much frequented by Cambridge folk who arrived there 'by fly', on bicycles, in punts or on foot. In May Week it opened at 6 a.m. and was the venue for fashionable breakfast parties *al fresco* in full evening dress.

In December 1910, complaining to his mother that 'horrible people' had appeared at the Orchard, Brooke moved next door to the Old Vicarage, renting from the Neeves two rooms on the ground floor and one on the first floor, with full board for thirty shillings a week. He formed a deep attachment to Grantchester, its trees, its meadows, the river in which he frequently bathed, and particularly the house itself, of which he wrote to Erica Cotterill: 'This is a deserted, lonely, dank, ruined, overgrown, gloomy, lovely house: with a garden to match. It is all five hundred years old, and fusty with the ghosts of generations of mouldering clergymen. It is a fit place to write my kind of poetry in . . .'

Lytton Strachey received a similarly lyrical account: 'The garden is the great glory. There is a soft lawn with a sundial and tangled, antique flowers abundantly; and a sham ruin, quite in a corner; built fifty years ago by Mr Shuckburgh, historian and rector of Grant-chester . . . There are trees rather too closely all round; and a mist.' Brooke's 'Mr Shuckburgh' may well have been Dr E. S. Shuck-burgh, classical historian and former Fellow and Librarian of Emmanuel College, who had lived in Grove Cottage in the village until his death in 1906.

At the Old Vicarage, Brooke worked on poems to be included in the first anthology of Georgian Poetry, a joint venture instigated by Edward Marsh, among which was to be included *The Old Vicarage, Grantchester*. His main commitment, however, was to his Fellowship dissertation on John Webster (1580–1625), a pioneer work which led to notable revivals by the Marlowe Dramatic Society. According to 'To An Unknown God', Reginald Pole's lightly fictionalised unpublished account of his friendship with Brooke, 'open books, magazines and miscellaneous manuscript papers were littered in profusion in every conceivable accommodation' in Brooke's study, now a drawing room, on the ground floor of the Old Vicarage.

The front of the Old Vicarage.

Brooke in the garden of the Old Vicarage.

While based in Grantchester, Brooke travelled quite widely in Europe, paying several visits to Berlin and staying in Munich for a few months on two occasions, the second time living with Ka. In England, he continued to be involved with the Fabians, but early relationships with the Bloomsbury set deteriorated. He quarrelled violently with Lytton Strachey and rejected the Bloomsbury code of behaviour. After he gained his fellowship at King's at the second attempt, in 1913, he travelled extensively in America and Canada and as far afield as Tahiti.

When war broke out in 1914, Brooke was anxious to enlist. Edward Marsh, by then private secretary to Winston Churchill, First Lord of the Admiralty, had introduced Brooke to the London literary and political scene, and through Churchill's influence Brooke obtained a commission in the newly created Royal Naval Division, nicknamed Winston's Wandering Wonders. Training at Betteshanger Park, he heard a rumour that the Old Vicarage was to be demolished, and dashed off an agitated note to Frances Cornford about it: 'Awful rumours prevail here that the Old Vicarage is to be destroyed. I wonder if you could find out if that's so; by whose orders; & what steps could be taken in the way of saving it. I mean, could one buy it, or the land? It seems to me very important. Failing that, I want some decent painter to make a picture of it (I hear Dent has got some hack to paint it.) And if there are any good

Sub-Lieutenant Rupert Brooke, Royal Naval Division, 1914.

photographers about, you might turn them on.' A fortnight later, he was writing in relief to E. J. Dent, the King's musicologist, 'Your scare . . . that the O.V. was to be demolished, proves unfounded. It shall yet be left for that slower Prussian, Time, to reduce it. Perhaps I may buy it with my prize money, after the war.'

In March 1915, after a field day on the Aegean island of Skyros while on his way with his battalion to Gallipoli, Brooke received a letter from Edward Marsh telling him that on Easter Sunday Dr Inge, Dean of St Paul's, had read from the pulpit excerpts from *The Soldier* ('If I should die, think only this of me'). A fortnight later, Brooke had a relapse of a fever which he had contracted together with dysentery when his ship had been diverted to Egypt and he had visited Cairo. After the field day, a mosquito bite on his lip became inflamed; secondary blood poisoning ensued and quickly proved fatal. He died on 23 April and was buried on Skyros in a peaceful and beautiful olive grove in which he and his friends had rested on the ill-fated field day.

Wood engraving of the Old Vicarage by Noel Rooke.

By the end of the war to end all wars, Rupert's formidable mother, Mary Ruth, had lost all three of her sons. It was she who put his intention to buy the Old Vicarage into effect by purchasing the freehold and bequeathing it, in memory of Rupert, to his close undergraduate friend Dudley Ward. The house was to stay in the Ward family until 1979, when the news that it was on the market for the first time in 65 years inspired this in Roger Woddis, writing for *Punch*:

> Ah God! to see the vampires stir
> To get their claws on Grantchester!
> And all the fans who've long forgotten
> The days when I was sent up rotten –
> And oh! to hear the Japanese
> Bidding on their tiny knees!
> Say, are there Arabs, cash in hand,

Come hotfoot from the Holy Land?
And do the rip-off merchants dream
Of flogging Youth and soft ice-cream?
And will the Vicarage, when sold,
Be modernised and called 'Ye Olde'?
Will there be takeaways to see
From Haslingfield to Madingley?
Will gentle ladies look forlorn
At finding all that Beauty gorn?
Oh, is the littered driveway full
Of coachloads down from Liverpool?
And do they drink – and void – their fill
Into the mill, into the mill?
Say, is there Piety yet to find,
Or has the Rural Dean resigned?
Love they the Good, or are they set
On living off my name? . . . oh! yet
Have they gone made in selling me?
And is there Brooke Bond now for tea?

The Old Vicarage from the back garden.

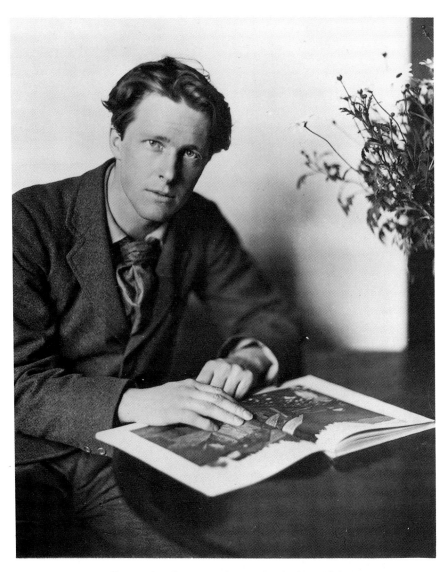

Rupert Brooke, 1913, *photographed by Sherril Schell.*

Brooke wrote *The Old Vicarage, Grantchester* in Berlin in May 1912 in a mood of considerable world weariness and frustration. The first part of his year had been unsuccessful; he had failed to obtain his Fellowship at King's, and his relationship with Ka Cox was imposing great stress on both of them. In Berlin before the marriage of Dudley Ward to his German bride Annemarie von der Planitz, Brooke was out of love with Germany and the Germans and homesick for England and the Old Vicarage. 'I've a fancy you may be, just now, in Grantchester,' he wrote to Ka. 'That river and the chestnuts – come back to me a lot.' At his habitual table in the Café des Westens in Charlottenburg, Brooke scribbled in pencil on four

Horsechestnuts at Grantchester, 1937, by Gwen Raverat.

small sheets of paper the first draft of the poem which was to become *The Old Vicarage, Grantchester*, although that was not the immediate choice of title. First entitled *Home*, it became *Fragments from a Poem to be Entitled 'The Sentimental Exile'*, and was published under that title in the June 1912 issue of the King's College undergraduate magazine *Basileon*. It was at the suggestion of Edward Marsh that Brooke changed the title to *The Old Vicarage, Grantchester*. Thus it appeared in the November 1912 issue of the *Poetry Review*, and thus it has remained.

The poem is constructed in octosyllabics or more precisely in iambic tetrameter couplets. The short lines trip off the tongue and are well suited to Brooke's purpose of expressing his yearning, masked in part in banter and satire, for home.

Just now the lilac is in bloom,
All before my little room;
And in my flower-beds, I think,
Smile the carnation and the pink;
And down the borders, well I know,
The poppy and the pansy blow . . .
Oh! there the chestnuts, summer through,

Beside the river make for you
A tunnel of green gloom, and sleep
Deeply above; and green and deep
The stream mysterious glides beneath,
Green as a dream and deep as death.
– Oh, damn! I know it! And I know
How the May fields all golden show,
And when the day is young and sweet,
Gild gloriously the bare feet
That run to bathe . . . .

The chestnuts, with the exception of one or two casualties of old age and high winds, stand as Brooke described them by the Mill Stream (a leat off the Granta) at the end of the garden. But the stream is hardly now as 'deep as death' – on a good day one can get across dry in waders. However, Brooke may not be taking poetic licence here because the river level was higher in his day, and the plains of Grantchester Meadows correspondingly more often flooded, before the sluice was put in downstream at Scudamore's boatyard. The flowers – lilac, poppies, pansies, pinks – still grow in the garden, nurtured out of piety; they flower around May, the month in which Brooke wrote the poem. But in 1912 the May fields showed golden with buttercups, not rape.

The Mill Stream rejoins the river Granta just below the Old Vicarage. A further short distance downstream there is a broad stretch close to the old cricket pitch where the river bed is gravelly. This used to be a favourite bathing spot for the village but few venture into the river there now, although gentlemen still disport themselves in the buff at the University Bathing Club downstream near Paradise Island.

There follows the section in which Brooke contrasts the stifling militarism of Prussian Berlin *here* in which he sits writing with his remembered vision of arcadian Grantchester *there*.

> *Du lieber Gott!*
> Here am I, sweating, sick, and hot,
> And there the shadowed waters fresh
> Lean up to embrace the naked flesh.

Temperamentvoll German Jews
Drink beer around; – and *there* the dews
Are soft beneath a morn of gold.
Here tulips bloom as they are told;
Unkempt about those hedges blows
An English unofficial rose;
And there the unregulated sun
Slopes down to rest when day is done,
And wakes a vague unpunctual star,
A slippered Hesper; and there are
Meads towards Haslingfield and Coton
Where *das Betreten*'s not *verboten* . . . .

Here is the line which gave Iris Murdoch the title of her novel *An Unofficial Rose* (probably the native dog-rose, but Brooke may have had in mind an exuberant *Rosa filipes* which until recently ramped over and through a cypress outside his study window in Grantchester), and the sunset correctly placed between Haslingfield and Madingley, which lie in an arc to the west of Grantchester. The line about the forbidden German grass evolved from at least two earlier versions. In *Basileon* it reads 'That are not *polizei verboten*', and in one copy of the magazine Brooke has altered it to: 'Whose *treten* is not *strengst verboten*'.

The next lines remind us that Brooke read the Classical Tripos at Cambridge. He starts off, but fortunately does not continue, in Greek with the tag εἴθε γενοίμην, first person aorist optative, and himself immediately provides the translation 'would I were'.

εἴθε γενοίμην . . . would I were
In Grantchester, in Grantchester! –
Some, it may be, can get in touch
With Nature there, or Earth, or such.
And clever modern men have seen
A Faun a-peeping through the green,
And felt the Classics were not dead,
To glimpse a Naiad's reedy head,
Or hear the Goat-foot piping low; . . .

In these allusions to naiads, fauns and the Goat-foot (the god Pan), Brooke is flirting with Paganism; Morgan Forster's early short stories and Kenneth Grahame's *The Wind in the Willows* embrace a similar slightly whimsical pagan mythology. Brooke was an energetic member of the fledgling Georgian Poetry group, named in honour of the new King George V, who had ascended the throne in 1910. The Georgians included John Drinkwater, James Elroy Flecker, Walter de la Mare, John Masefield and Wilfred Gibson, and a romantic streak of paganism also suffuses some of their work. But in the next section of the poem, Brooke dismisses the *clever modern men* and their fantasies, and recalls his own idyllic days at Grantchester –

But these are things I do not know.
I only know that you may lie
Day long and watch the Cambridge sky,

And, flower-lulled in sleepy grass,
Hear the cool lapse of hours pass,
Until the centuries blend and blur
In Grantchester, in Grantchester . . . .
Still in the dawnlit waters cool
His ghostly Lordship swims his pool,
And tries the strokes, essays the tricks,
Long learnt on Hellespont, or Styx,
Dan Chaucer hears his river still
Chatter beneath a phantom mill.
Tennyson notes, with studious eye,
How Cambridge waters hurry by . . . .

This passage reflects, not for the first time in the poem, Brooke's passion for bathing; later, in a war sonnet, he was to salute the soldiers dying in the trenches as 'swimmers into cleanness leaping'. Reports of swimming recur in friends' accounts of visits to Grantchester. On one warm moonlit night in 1911 during her stay at the Old Vicarage, Brooke took Virginia Stephen (later Woolf) upstream to Byron's Pool. 'Let's go swimming, quite naked,' he said, and they did. Virginia was disappointed that her London circle remained calm at news of the incident, though it may have contributed to the nickname of Neo-Pagans which Bloomsbury conferred on Brooke and his Cambridge friends.

In the same summer David Garnett trod the same path with Brooke. 'We went about midnight – for I had arrived rather late,' he wrote, 'to bathe in Byron's Pool. We walked out of the garden of the Old Vicarage into the lane full of thick white dust, which slipped under our weight as we walked noiselessly in our sandshoes, and then through the dew-soaked grass of the meadow over the mill-wall leading to the pool, to bathe naked in the unseen water, smelling of wild peppermint and mud.'

Brooke's allusions to three poets with Cambridge connexions may all be linked to Byron's Pool, which lies about half a mile upstream of the Old Vicarage, above a dam near the boundary between Trumpington and Grantchester. The first allusion, to the ghostly Lord swimming his pool, is easy. Byron swam the Hellespont in 1810, and presumably in due course the Styx as well. He had come up to Trinity College, Cambridge in 1805 and there is a legend, although no documentary evidence, that he swam in the pool that now bears his name. Widnall in his *Reminiscences of Trumpington Fifty Years Ago*, published in 1889, refers to one of his favourite childhood walks as being through Byron's Grove and round by Grantchester, which may confirm that Byron's Pool was so called in the 1830s, though it is not named on the Baker map of Cambridge of 1821.

Brooke's next poetical allusion is little harder. Dan Chaucer is not the little-known brother of the great Geoffrey; *dan* is a normal mediaeval contraction for *dominus*. The 'phantom mill' is the old mill which used to stand at Byron's Pool, and the allusion is to *The Reeve's Tale*:

> At Trumpingtoun not fer fro Cantebrigge
> Ther goth a brook and over that a brigge:
> Upon the whiche brook ther stonte a mylle.
> And this is very sooth that I you telle.

The last allusion, to Tennyson, is the most problematic. Brooke knew his Tennyson well, although it was then fashionable to deride this great Victorian poet. Convalescing in Italy in 1905, Brooke complained to the young Geoffrey Keynes: 'The only things to read in this benighted place are Tennyson's Poems and a London Directory of 1888. I've tried them both and prefer the latter.'

Tennyson, says Brooke, 'notes, with studious eye, How Cambridge waters hurry by' but he does not seem to have done so in as many words. Tennyson wrote two poems about Cambridge but neither of them mentions water, though Graham Chainey in his *Literary History of Cambridge* sees the Cam as being the model for the river in *The Lady of Shalott*. Christopher Ricks suggests that the allusion is to Tennyson's poem *The Miller's Daughter*, which has a loose Cambridge connexion, for of this tale of a miller and his family, Tennyson wrote, 'No particular mill, but if I thought at all of any mill, it was that of Trumpington, near Cambridge.'

> I loved the brimming wave that swam
> Through quiet meadows round the mill,
> The sleepy pool above the dam,
> The pool beneath it never still.

Arthur Mee, in *The King's England* for Cambridgeshire, also linked *The Miller's Daughter* to Trumpington Mill. Further, one of Widnall's small books is entitled *'The Miller's Daughter'* and is a fanciful account of the life and times of a fifteenth-century miller of Trumpington. If Brooke knew all – or even part – of this, then his reference to Tennyson, linked with Byron and Chaucer to Byron's Pool and the old Trumpington Mill, is an admirably tidy one.

Next come the spectral vicars and the dusty curates, in an obvious reference to the house's 150-year history as a vicarage.

> And in that garden, black and white,
> Creep whispers through the grass all night;
> And spectral dance, before the dawn,
> A hundred Vicars down the lawn;

> Curates, long dust, will come and go
> On lissom, clerical, printless toe;
> And oft between the boughs is seen

The sly shade of a Rural Dean . . . .
Till, at a shiver in the skies,
Vanishing with Satanic cries,
The prim ecclesiastic rout
Leaves but a startled sleeper-out,
Grey heavens, the first bird's drowsy calls,
The falling house that never falls.

Brooke himself, with his Neo-Pagan fondness for camping and sleeping out of doors, is the startled sleeper-out. 'The falling house' is rather hard to place. Probably it is the Old Vicarage itself, viewed from the verandah, where the prevailing east wind creates the illusion that the house is falling towards one. Perhaps it is Widnall's Castle which trails off into a contrived romantic ruin at its easterly end. Or, as casual visitors sometimes suppose, is it the Garner Cottages between the Old Vicarage and the Mill, which have a gable end that leans markedly towards the road?

Brooke's nostalgia hardens into a resolve to go home to join the 'men with Splendid Hearts', an ironic line later made grave by its inscription on the War Memorial in Grantchester churchyard.

God! I will pack, and take a train,
And get me to England once again!
For England's the one land, I know,
Where men with Splendid Hearts may go;
And Cambridgeshire, of all England,
The shire for Men who Understand;
And of *that* district I prefer
The lovely hamlet Grantchester.

For Cambridge people rarely smile,
Being urban, squat, and packed with guile;
And Royston men in the far South
Are black and fierce and strange of mouth;
At Over they fling oaths at one,
And worse than oaths at Trumpington,
And Ditton girls are mean and dirty,
And there's none in Harston under thirty,
And folks in Shelford and those parts
Have twisted lips and twisted hearts,
And Barton men make Cockney rhymes,
And Coton's full of nameless crimes,
And things are done you'd not believe
At Madingley, on Christmas Eve.
Strong men have run for miles and miles,
When one from Cherry Hinton smiles;
Strong men have blanched, and shot their wives,
Rather than send them to St Ives;
Strong men have cried like babes, bydam,
To hear what happened at Babraham.

Brooke slips up slightly on topographical detail: Royston is in
Hertfordshire (though it was in part in Cambridgeshire until about
1888) and St Ives was in the old Huntingdonshire although it is now
indeed in Cambridgeshire. In the first draft of the poem, the
candidate village names are written in the margin and appear to
have been chosen more for convenient scansion than for any
accurate local allusion, though the Cockney rhymes made by
Barton men may refer to the anonymous ballad *The Knocking
Ghost of Barton*, the refrain of which reads:

Jiminy, criminy, what a lark,
You must not stir out after dark,
For if you do you'll get a mark –
     From this knocking ghost of Barton.

There is no documentary evidence for unbelievable happenings
at Madingley, but Brooke may have known of a village myth that
held that the High Church late-nineteenth-century Rector of Mad-

ingley promised a High Mass on Christmas Eve. The squire forbade his tenants to attend but they went, defiantly, and were turned out of their homes on Christmas Day. They slept for a while on the Rectory floor but then the Rector's wife, who was well off, bought the houses up along the Avenue for them to live in.

Brooke's tour of Cambridgeshire has proved particularly irresistible to parodists. Here is Robert Smith in the *Cambridge Evening News*, hitting back on behalf of the slighted women of the county:

> O who can look and not feel smitten
> With the wenches of Fen Ditton,
> Or spurn that motherly allure
> Of Harston ladies more mature?

Nevill Willmer's 1981 parody takes a more scientific line, with references to the Animal Physiology Laboratory at Babraham, the test-tube baby clinic at Bourn Hall and the five-kilometre telescope at the nearby village of Barton.

> Test tubes have nurtured lambs (no dam)
> In laboratories at Babraham,
> And in the ancient halls at Bourn
> To sterile couples babes are born.
> *Sic transit gloria mundi* here
> In Grantchester, in Grantchester!
> Where clever men may now commune
> With black holes, galaxies or moon . . . .

After his mockery of the villages, Brooke comes with an exaggerated sigh of relief to Grantchester . . . .

> But Grantchester! ah, Grantchester!
> There's peace and holy quiet there,
> Great clouds along pacific skies,
> And men and women with straight eyes,
> Lithe children lovelier than a dream,
> A bosky wood, a slumbrous stream,
> And little kindly winds that creep
> Round twilight corners, half asleep.
> In Grantchester their skins are white;
> They bathe by day, they bathe by night;

The women there do all they ought;
The men observe the Rules of Thought.
They love the Good; they worship Truth;
They laugh uproariously in youth;
(And when they get to feeling old,
They up and shoot themselves, I'm told) . . . .

In the margin of the first draft of the poem there are four
further lines in the same vein, excised from later versions, which
perhaps bear the faint imprint of Brooke's espousal of Fabianism:

And so at General Elections
They have the strength of their convictions;
The atheists vote Liberal
And many do not vote at all.

Finally Brooke casts away his mask of playfulness and declares
himself in the deeply felt coda.

Ah God! to see the branches stir
Across the moon at Grantchester!

To smell the thrilling-sweet and rotten
Unforgettable, unforgotten
River-smell, and hear the breeze
Sobbing in the little trees.

Say, do the elm-clumps greatly stand,
Still guardians of that holy land?
The chestnuts shade, in reverend dream,
The yet unacademic stream?

Is dawn a secret shy and cold
Anadyomene, silver-gold?
And sunset still a golden sea
From Haslingfield to Madingley?

Anadyomene (pronounced anna-die-ómeny) means emergent, here presumably dawn emergent from the night. The Granta is an 'unacademic stream' because it is upstream of the university city, in which it goes by the name of the Cam. The most notable elm clumps were at the north end of the village, but sadly they no longer greatly stand, having fallen victim to the elm-bark beetle.

> And after, ere the night is born,
> Do hares come out about the corn?
> Oh, is the water sweet and cool,
> Gentle and brown, above the pool?
> And laughs the immortal river still
> Under the mill, under the mill?

The old mill at Grantchester, burnt down in 1928.

The mill to which Brooke here refers is not the 'phantom mill' at Byron's Pool in Trumpington, but rather Grantchester Mill, an eighteenth-century mill owned by Merton College, Oxford. In Brooke's day this straddled the Mill Stream above the Mill Pool, a short distance upstream of the Old Vicarage. Grantchester Mill burned down in 1928 and has been rebuilt as a private house under which the river still laughs.

> Say, is there Beauty yet to find?
> And Certainty? and Quiet kind?

Deep meadows yet, for to forget
The lies, and truths, and pain? . . . oh! yet
Stands the Church clock at ten to three?
And is there honey still for tea?

In the first draft of the poem, the Church clock stood at half past three, and it is not known why Brooke changed it in the final version: possibly because ten to three is lighter in rhythm. There is in Grantchester a vague reminiscence that the clock was not working in Brooke's day, but it is not thought to have stood at ten to three, or indeed at half past three; Lady Tansley's recollection was that it was stopped at a quarter to eight. In Widnall's model of the church, the clock's hands stand at ten past three, a tantalising near miss.

The 'honey for tea' probably alludes to Henry Neeve's hobby of bee-keeping; his honey was on sale at the Orchard Tea Rooms next door to the Old Vicarage. When Brooke arrived back in the Old Vicarage in July 1912, he was amused to discover that Florence Neeve had seen his poem in *Basileon*. 'You see,' said she, bringing in the tea-tray on his first afternoon at home, 'there *is* honey still for tea!' The poem had only just made the June issue of *Basileon*. The editor had written to Brooke in hope of a contribution, and asked the printer to hold his hand in response to Brooke's telegraphed reply: 'A masterpiece is on its way.'

That then is the poem, the hymn to England which Brooke wrote in Berlin, the piece for which he was awarded a useful prize of £30 for the best poem in the previous year's *Poetry Review* by his fellow poet Edward Thomas. Brooke was a stern critic of his own poetry, though not quite so stern as some have been since, dismissing much of it as 'unimportant prettiness'. He hated the thought of being categorised as a minor poet – might as well talk of a minor rose or a minor sunset, he said. If Brooke is a minor poet, this 'long lanky lax-limbed set of verses' (his own description), this 'adorably whimsical lyric' (Henry James's) is surely as good as a minor poem can be. May the pulse in the eternal mind that is Rupert Brooke rest in peace, and in the 'lovely hamlet' long may his memory be green!

And get me to England once again!
For England's the one land, I know,
Where men with Splendid Hearts may go;
And Cambridgeshire, of all England,
The shire for Men who Understand;
And of that district I prefer
The lovely hamlet, Grantchester.

For Cambridge people rarely smile,
Being urban, squat, and packed with guile;
And Royston men in the far south
Are black and fierce and strange of mouth;
At Over they fling ~~oaths~~ oaths at one,
And worse than oaths at Trumpington.
And Ditton girls are mean and dirty,
And there's none in Harston under thirty,
And folks in Shelford and those parts
Have twisted lips and twisted hearts,
And Barton men make cockney rhymes,
And Coton's full of nameless crimes,
And things are done you'd not believe
At Madingley on Christmas Eve.
Strong men have run for miles and miles,
When one from Cherry Hinton smiles;
Strong men have blanched, and shot their wives,
Rather than send them to St Ives;
Strong men have cried like babes, bydam,
To hear what happened at Babraham.
But Grantchester! ah, Grantchester!
There's peace and holy quiet there,
Great clouds along pacific skies,
And men and women with straight eyes,
Little children lovelier than a dream,
A bosky wood, a slumbrous stream,
And little kindly winds that creep
Round twilight corners, half-asleep.
In Grantchester their skins are white,